SOCCER STARS

MARTA

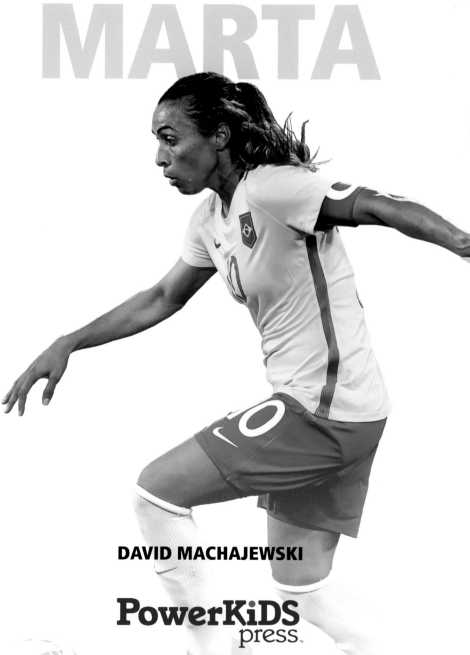

DAVID MACHAJEWSKI

PowerKiDS
press™

New York

Published in 2019 by The Rosen Publishing Group, Inc.
29 East 21st Street, New York, NY 10010

First Edition

Editor: Elizabeth Krajnik
Book Design: Michael Flynn

Photo Credits: Cover (Marta), pp. 1, 5 Stuart Franklin - FIFA/FIFA/Getty Images; cover (stadium background) winui/Shutterstock.com; cover (player glow) Nejron Photo/Shutterstock.com; pp. 3, 23, 24 (background) Narong Jongsirikul/Shutterstock.com; pp. 4–6, 8–10, 12, 14, 16–18, 20, 22 (ball background) DRN Studio/Shutterstock.com; pp. 4, 21 Icon Sportswire/Getty Images; p. 7 NurPhoto/Getty Images; p. 8 Filipe Frazao/Shutterstock.com; p. 9 Buda Mendes/Getty Images Sport/Getty Images; p. 10 Luis Louro/Shutterstock.com; p. 11 Doug Pensinger/Getty Images Sport/Getty Images; p. 13 Michael Steele/Getty Images Sport/Getty Images; p. 15 Mike Zarrilli/Getty Images Sport/Getty Images; p. 17 Clive Rose - FIFA/FIFA/Getty Images; p. 18 Matthew Lewis - FIFA/FIFA/Getty Images; p. 19 Anadolu Agency/Getty Images; p. 20 Mapics/Shutterstock.com; p. 22 Mike Hewitt - FIFA/FIFA/Getty Images.

Cataloging-in-Publication Data

Names: Machajewski, David .
Title: Marta / David Machajewski.
Description: New York : PowerKids Press, 2019. | Series: Soccer stars | Includes glossary and index.
Identifiers: ISBN 9781538345108 (pbk.) | ISBN 9781538343524 (library bound) | ISBN 9781538345115 (6 pack)
Subjects: LCSH: Vieira, Marta, 1986–Juvenile literature. | Women soccer players–Brazil–Biography–Juvenile literature.
Classification: LCC GV942.7.V515 M34 2019 | DDC 796.334092 B–dc23

Manufactured in the United States of America

CPSIA Compliance Information: Batch #CWPK19 For Further Information contact Rosen Publishing, New York, New York at 1-800-237-9932

CONTENTS

MEET MARTA. 4

EARLY YEARS 6

DRIVEN TO GREATNESS 8

RISING STAR 10

MAKING HISTORY 12

MOVE TO THE
    UNITED STATES 14

RETURN TO SWEDEN. 16

OFF THE FIELD 18

FUTEBOL, FOTBOLL, SOCCER. . 20

WORLD'S GREATEST. 22

GLOSSARY 23

INDEX. 24

WEBSITES 24

MEET MARTA

If someone asked you what the world's most popular sport is, what would you say? If you're from the United States, you might answer baseball or basketball. However, in most countries there's no game more popular than soccer. Soccer, which is known as football in most countries, has more fans around the world than any other sport.

CONNECTING WITH FANS IS AN IMPORTANT PART OF BEING A SOCCER STAR. MANY YOUNG SOCCER PLAYERS LOOK UP TO MARTA.

Because soccer is such an important part of so many people's lives, it takes a very special person to become a soccer star. Marta Vieira da Silva, known simply as Marta, is often considered the greatest female soccer player of all time.

STAR POWER

Brazilian—and sometimes Portuguese, Spanish, and Angolan—soccer players often go by a single name. Calling someone by his or her first name or nickname is more personal than calling them by his or her last name.

EARLY YEARS

Marta was born on February 19, 1986, in the city of Dois Riachos in the Brazilian state of Alagoas. Marta began playing soccer with other children in the streets of her neighborhood. However, many of the boys didn't like losing to a girl and treated her poorly.

In Brazil, many people thought girls shouldn't play soccer. Even Marta's family didn't approve of her playing soccer. However, she continued playing. When Marta was 14 years old, she went to Rio de Janeiro to try out for Vasco da Gama's women's squad. She played with Vasco da Gama for two years and then played with Santa Cruz.

STAR POWER

In Brazil, the government banned women from playing sports that were "incompatible [not fitting] with their nature" from 1941 until 1979. Even though the ban has been lifted, women's sports in Brazil still aren't treated with the same respect as men's sports.

MARTA PLAYED IN AN ALL-MALE LEAGUE, WHICH HELPED HER SKILLS IMPROVE AND TAUGHT HER HOW TO HANDLE UNFAIR TREATMENT FOR BEING A FEMALE SOCCER PLAYER.

DRIVEN TO GREATNESS

Vasco da Gama was a **professional** soccer team. Marta's relationship with Helena Pacheco, her coach at Vasco, had a great impact on her life and **career**. Helena recalls that, as a young player, Marta was very determined and focused. When Marta was just 15 years old, she played in her first Brazilian **championship** game and was chosen as the best player.

SINCE THE BEGINNING OF HER CAREER, MARTA HAS STOOD OUT AS A GREAT PLAYER WHO HAS HELPED HER TEAMS WIN MANY GAMES AND CHAMPIONSHIPS.

However, after a year and a half, Vasco's president cut the women's team. Marta didn't want to go back to Dois Riachos. She decided to play **futsal** on the weekends to make a little bit of money.

STAR POWER

Even though Marta was a professional soccer player, female soccer players didn't make much money at the time. Marta would send any money she made back to her mother in Dois Riachos.

RISING STAR

In 2002, Marta was named to the Brazilian national under-19 team, which qualified for the Fédéracion Internacionale de Football Association (FIFA) Under-19 Women's World Championship held in Canada.

Even though Brazil took fourth place, Marta won the Silver Ball, which is given to the second-best player in the tournament. She was the fourth-highest scorer of the tournament with six goals. Marta was also named to the all-star team as a forward.

In 2003, Marta was called up to the **senior** national team, which qualified for the FIFA Women's World Cup held in the United States. Brazil was eliminated in the quarterfinals, but Marta scored three goals throughout the tournament.

EVEN THOUGH BRAZIL LOST TO SWEDEN IN THE 2003 FIFA WOMEN'S WORLD CUP, MARTA EARNED A SPOT ON THE MASTERCARD ALL-STAR TEAM AS A SUBSTITUTE MIDFIELDER.

MAKING HISTORY

When Marta was just 17 years old, she received a call from the president of Umeå IK, a Swedish professional soccer club. The club wanted to sign her to play for their team. She was the first Brazilian woman to play professional soccer in Europe.

While playing for Umeå, Marta helped the team win the 2004 Union of European Football Associations (UEFA) Women's Cup. In 2007 and 2008, Umeå reached the UEFA Women's Cup finals, but didn't win. Marta also helped Umeå win four Damallsvenskan championships in a row! The team also won the Svenska Cupen in 2007. Marta was the league's top scorer in 2004, 2005, and 2008.

STAR POWER

While playing for Umeå, Marta also helped the Brazilian team win silver medals at the 2004 Summer Olympics in Athens, Greece, and the 2008 Summer Olympics in Beijing, China.

FROM 2006 TO 2010, MARTA WAS NAMED FIFA WORLD PLAYER OF THE YEAR FIVE TIMES IN A ROW.

MOVE TO THE UNITED STATES

In 2009, Marta left Europe to play for Women's Professional Soccer's Los Angeles Sol. That season, she won the PUMA Golden Boot award for being the league's top scorer, and she was named the WPS Most Valuable Player. She also helped the Sol reach the WPS Championship Final.

Marta went to play for the FC Gold Pride of Santa Clara, California. For the second year in a row, Marta was named WPS MVP and won the PUMA Golden Boot. She helped lead the FC Gold Pride to the WPS Championship and was named the MVP of the WPS Championship.

STAR POWER

During the WPS off-seasons in 2009 and 2010, Marta played with Santos FC, a Brazilian soccer club. In 2009, the club won the Copa Libertadores de Fútbol and the Copa do Brasil.

IN 2011, MARTA JOINED THE WPS WESTERN NEW YORK FLASH. SHE WON THE PUMA GOLDEN BOOT FOR THE THIRD YEAR IN A ROW. THAT SEASON, MARTA HELPED THE FLASH WIN THE WPS CHAMPIONSHIP.

RETURN TO SWEDEN

On February 22, 2012, Marta returned to Sweden to play for Damallsvenskan club Tyresö FF. That season, Tyresö won its first Damallsvenskan title. In July 2014, Marta began playing for Damallsvenskan club FC Rosengård. The team won the Damallsvenskan title in 2014 and 2015, the Svenska Cupen in 2016, and the Svenska Supercupen in 2015 and 2016. In March 2017, Marta became a Swedish **citizen**.

After Rosengård lost to Barcelona in the quarterfinals of the 2017 UEFA Women's Champions League, Marta signed a two-year **contract** with National Women's Soccer League (NWSL) team Orlando Pride. During her first season, Marta scored 13 goals, was named to the CONCACAF Female Best XI, and was selected to the NWSL Best XI.

DURING THE 2015 FIFA WOMEN'S WORLD CUP MATCH BETWEEN BRAZIL AND SOUTH KOREA, MARTA SCORED HER 15TH WORLD CUP GOAL, SETTING A NEW RECORD FOR THE MOST WORLD CUP GOALS SCORED IN HISTORY. THIS WAS HER FOURTH WORLD CUP.

STAR POWER

In 2007, Marta won the FIFA Women's World Cup Golden Ball and Golden Shoe awards. *Sports Illustrated* ranked Marta seventh in the Top 20 Female Athletes of the Decade (2000–2009). In 2016, she was named to FIFA FIFPro's World XI as a midfielder.

OFF THE FIELD

Many young girls interested in sports, especially in Brazil, look up to Marta as a role model. She has spent many years fighting the unfair treatment of women's sports in Brazil and unequal pay for female athletes.

Marta is an ambassador for FIFA Live Your Goals campaign, which helps give girls and women around the world the chance to play soccer at all levels in their home countries. On October 11, 2010, the United Nations Development Programme appointed Marta as a goodwill ambassador to help women achieve their dreams as a way to fight poverty, or the state of being poor.

ON MARCH 4, 2014, MARTA AND OTHER UNDP GOODWILL AMBASSADORS PLAYED IN THE 11TH MATCH AGAINST POVERTY, A **CHARITY** SOCCER MATCH FOR THE PHILIPPINES, AT STADE DE SUISSE IN BERN, SWITZERLAND.

FUTEBOL, FOTBOLL, SOCCER

Because her career has taken her all around the world, Marta has had to move a lot. She often says she misses her family. Marta has two brothers and one sister, and she **dedicated** her 2011 Player of the Year award to them.

Marta's travels have also given her the chance to learn new languages. Because she was born and raised in Brazil, she speaks Portuguese, the official language of Brazil. When she moved to Sweden, she began learning Swedish. Today, Marta is **fluent** in Swedish. Since playing for a number of teams in the United States, Marta also speaks English.

STOCKHOLM, SWEDEN

MARTA PLANS ON LIVING IN SWEDEN AFTER SHE RETIRES, OR STOPS PLAYING SOCCER.

WORLD'S GREATEST

Today, Marta is known as one of the world's greatest soccer players—both male and female. She is the all-time leading goal scorer in Women's World Cup history with 15 World Cup goals. She has won five FIFA World Player of the Year awards in a row. Marta has earned the love of fans across the world for her incredible talent, dedication, and skill.

From the streets of Brazil to roaring stadiums across the globe, Marta's journey shows that hard work pays off and that you should never give up on what you believe in.

GLOSSARY

career: A period of time spent doing a job or activity.

championship: A contest to find out who's the best player or team in a sport.

charity: An organization or fund for helping the needy.

citizen: A person who legally belongs to a country and has the rights and protection of that country.

contract: A legal agreement between people, companies, and other groups.

dedicate: To say or write that something is written or performed as a compliment to someone.

fluent: Able to speak a language easily and very well.

futsal: A sport similar to soccer and played with five-person teams on a basketball-style court with no walls and a smaller, low-bouncing ball.

professional: Taking part in a sport to make money.

senior: Higher in standing or rank than another person or team in the same position.

INDEX

B
Brazil, 5, 6, 8, 10, 12, 14, 18, 20, 22

D
Damallsvenskan, 12, 16
Dois Riachos, 6, 9

F
FC Rosengård, 16
FIFA, 10, 17, 18, 22
futsal, 9

G
Golden Boot, 14
Golden Shoe, 17

L
Los Angeles Sol, 14

N
National Women's Soccer League (NWSL), 16

O
Olympic Games, 12
Orlando Pride, 16

P
Pacheco, Helena, 8
Player of the Year, 13, 20, 22

S
Santa Cruz, 6
Santos FC, 14
Silver Ball, 10
Svenska Cupen, 12, 16
Svenska Supercupen, 16
Sweden, 12, 16, 20, 21

T
Tyresö FF, 16

U
UEFA Women's Cup, 12, 16
Umeå IK, 12

V
Vasco da Gama, 6, 8–9

W
Western New York Flash, 15
World Cup, 10, 17, 22
World Player of the Year, 13
WPS Championship, 14

WEBSITES

Due to the changing nature of Internet links, PowerKids Press has developed an online list of websites related to the subject of this book. This site is updated regularly. Please use this link to access the list:
www.powerkidslinks.com/socstars/marta